Catching the Limit

Catching the Limit

Mark Thalman

Mark Thalman

NORTHWEST POETRY SERIES

FAIRWEATHER PRESS • BROWNSVILLE, OREGON

First Edition 2 3 4 5 6 7 8 9

Library of Congress Cataloging in Publication Data
Mark Thalman, Catching the Limit
ISBN 13: 978-0-9822982-0-6
Library of Congress Control Number: 2009921309

Fairweather Books is an imprint of Bedbug Press

Author photo: Carole Thalman
Front Cover: *Descending–Osprey*, 30" x 40", acrylic on canvas, 2004,
    © Robert Bateman. Reproduction rights courtesy of Robert M. Bateman,
    Boshkung, Inc.
Cover Design: Cheryl McLean

Printed by Thomson-Shore, Inc., Dexter, Michigan

This book is printed on acid-free paper.

In memory of my parents and grandparents

ACKNOWLEDGMENTS

Some of these poems first appeared in the following publications
and later appeared in anthologies:

American Land Forum: "Mt. St. Helens: Inside the Blast Zone"
Anemone: "In the Silence of a Pine Cone Falling," "Mystery"
The Anthology of Eugene Writers, Northwest Review Books:
"Aerial Delivery: Bombing the Cascades"
Anthology of Magazine Verse & Yearbook of American Poetry, Monitor Book
Company: "Catching the Limit," "Oregon Rain," "Summit Lake"
Banyan Review: "Blowdown"
Blue Unicorn: "After the Downpour," "Blackberry Season," "Deer Among
Blue Woods," "Below Juniper Bend," "Homestead," "The Octopus Tree"
Caffeine Destiny: "Highway to the Coast"
Calussa Review: "Catching the Limit"
Carolina Quarterly: "Shelter Cove"
Chariton Review: "Cabin Fever," "Eagle Rock," "Mirror in the Forest,"
"Swallows at Walterville," "Thawing Out"
Croton Review: "Valsetz"
Deer Drink the Moon: Poems of Oregon, Ooligan Press, Portland State
University: "Born in Oregon," "Freezing Moon," "Highway to the Coast,"
"Midwinter: Sauvie Island," "North Umpqua, Summer Run,"
"Oregon Rain," "Swallows at Walterville"
Eighty on the Eighties: A Decade's History in Verse, The Ashland Poetry Press:
"Mt. St. Helens: Inside the Blast Zone"
Facets: "Full Moon, Clear Sky"
From Here We Speak: An Anthology of Oregon Poetry, Oregon State
University: "Catching the Limit"
Gin Bender Poetry Review: "North Umpqua, Summer Run"
The Great American Poetry Show: "Clear Lake"
Greenfield Review: "Nishawaka Creek"
Lactuca: "Painting the Boat"
MacGuffin: "Firewood"
Many Mountains Moving: "Encounter"
M Review: "Inheritance," "McKenzie River"
Natural Bridge: "Newport"

The Pacific: "Odell Lake"
Pearl: "Midwinter: Sauvie Island," "Uncle Eric's Fishing Tips,"
"What the River Gave Me"
Pendragon: "Westfir"
Pennsylvania Review: "Black Canyon"
Poetpourri: "Constructing Clocks," "Moving into Night"
Poetry Midwest: "Among These Hills"
Poetry Now: "Born in Oregon," "On the Dock at Evening"
Rocky Mountain Review: "Aerial Delivery: Bombing the Cascades,"
"Summit Lake"
Seems: "Church"
Snapdragon: "Clamming," "Siletz"
Spectrum: "Harvest"
Starting with Little Things, Oregon Arts Foundation: "Born in Oregon"
Texas Review: "Rough Wind"
Tree Magic, Sunshine Press Publications: "Freezing Moon"
Washout: "Oregon Rain"
Widner Review: "Freezing Moon"
Wisconsin Review: "In the Deschutes"
Writers' Dojo: "Serenity Bay, Odell Lake"
Xanadu: "If You Know Where to Look"

The last five lines of William Stafford's poem "In Oregon" originally appeared in the *Northwest Review*. Used by permission of the Estate of William Stafford.

Excerpt from *The Wilderness World of John Muir*, edited by Edwin Way Teale, renewed 1982 by Nellie D. Teale. Reprinted by permission of Houghton Mifflin Company. All rights reserved.

Special thanks go to Joseph Bruchac, Lars Nordstrom, Ralph Salisbury, and Ingrid Wendt for their wisdom and support. My sincere appreciation to the late Tony Gorsline and to Donn Gorsline for publishing these poems. Also, love to my wife, Carole, for all her help on this artistic journey.

CONTENTS

I. The Landscape

II. In the Cascades

I

The Landscape

You walk the vacant country, give
a look to anything that holds on.
Down a fence row your eyes come
to rest, far—a post, a post,
a tree, an old barn, rain.

William Stafford

WHAT THE RIVER GAVE ME

Along this beach,
the Columbia rounds and smoothes
agate, granite, and basalt.

I put in my knapsack
ones that remind me
of a speckled trout,
a piece of limburger cheese,
a shrimp-like embryo,
the moon, an eyeball,
a jelly bean pink with flecks
that sparkle like salmon scales,
a clamshell never to open,
a lump of calcified brain,
the molar from the jaw of a bear.

Turning them over again in my hands
I can feel their power . . .

born of fire,
bulldozed by glaciers,
abraded for a millennium
from pectoral fins
of migrating salmon.

When I get home,
I put them in a jar of water,
in the sun
in the kitchen windowsill,
so they may gleam
as in the moment I found them.

And on cold gray winter days,
these stones will take me back
through fragrant sweetgrass
and dried thistles
to that shore.

IF YOU KNOW WHERE TO LOOK

The trail running west to east
from the Willamette Valley
over the Santiam's Cascade crest
is a thin faint line,
a tan, sometimes brownish path,
where nothing grows,
since every spring
for thousands of years
after high snows melted
moccasins tread
footfall on footfall
along the same track
crossing from flood plains
and old-growth forests
to desert plateau
and lava flows
in search of obsidian.

Most of these ancient routes,
being the most efficient,
have been paved over
into state highways.
Cars and pickups
with Indian names
like Pontiac and Cheyenne
traveling faster than arrows.

VALSETZ

Out of the woods, a doe and fawn
self-consciously choose their way along
the slope of meadow to drink at the creek.

Steam rising from nostrils, sensing
a change in wind, they step lightly uphill,
blending into the solitude of trees.

A logging truck carrying a full load
explodes over the rise and continues
to thunder down the road
filling the void which was silence,
then fades, ebbing away . . .

leaving the land quiet—
the sort of stillness that follows
the report of a hunter's gun.

Among these hills, rusting barbwire fences:
posts gray as weathered granite,
not keeping anyone or anything
from going where they please.

CHURCH

This country church
with its one room and steeple,
boards bleached to bone,
endures by the dirt road.

For miles around,
stalks of ripe wheat bow their heads.

Anyone is welcome here.
The last minister had the doors unhinged
and carted away.

Now, white pigeons roost in the belfry.
When the spirit moves, they burst like shot:
a choir of wings, afternoon thunder, angels
into the blue again.

HOMESTEAD

Sun slants across the evening fields
embellishing a gray barn. I walk with my wife
to the farmhouse where she was born.
The windows are small and dark with dust.

Held captive by blackberry vines,
a tractor grows rust. Our shadows flow in front of us
like the first water of a stream spilling down a hill.

We hold hands.
Swallows sporadically call through the dimming light.
At night deer browse the tangled orchard
for ripening apples.

SWALLOWS AT WALTERVILLE

Not until the sun begins to set in align
with the large willow, pump house
and back porch, do they return.

Their clamor disrupting the stillness
of the plowed fields, I raise my head:
memory jolted; the song remembered
I was not aware I had forgotten.

I walk to the side of the barn,
take out my pocketknife
and carve the date into a plank
that is the calendar of their arrival
for the past twenty years.

From this time forward, each rain turns warmer.
The river courses high with a heavy runoff of snow.
I will begin planting cabbage and sweet corn tomorrow.

BELOW JUNIPER BEND

The cabin extends out from the bank
so it rests on two creosote pilings
that are slim and long and wading
in the shallows
like the legs
of a blue heron.

An old Indian built the place
next to where a stream
plunges, stair stepping down
the mountainside,
branching into the Umpqua.
More agile than even a bear's paw,
he would dip what looked to be
a butterfly net, only stronger,
and draw up salmon.

After he died, the land sold
to a thin, gray haired woman,
who will shoot and skin you
same as any raccoon
after her fish. Above the mantel
hangs a Confederate rifle
her father carried in the war.

All day she sits rocking in the kitchen window
with needles and red yarn,
watching the steelhead knit
across the bottom
as she knits for the coming winter . . .
amused like a cat
that can't get at them,
but is somehow reassured
they will be there
whenever she lifts her gaze.

HIGHWAY TO THE COAST

Thick and green, the hills rise
on each other's shoulders.

High ridges disappear in fog
make me wish I was born of water.

At the divide, I taste the cool ocean air,
the way a deer finds a salt lick,

and roller-coaster down a narrow road
that does not believe in a straight line.

Blackberry vines
crawl through barbed wire fences.

Small towns occur like a whim.
As if in a coma, they merely survive.

I tune in the only station
and listen to country-western.

Static gradually drowns the singer out.
Rounding a corner, he pops to the surface

for another breath,
simply to sink back still singing.

Fir shadows lace the road.
Bracken cascades embankments.

At the next curve, a farmhouse is half finished—
boards weathered raw. Chickens roost in a gutted Chevy.

Scattered among these hills, families
rely on small private lumber mills,

the disability or unemployment check,
the killing of an out of season elk.

NORTH UMPQUA, SUMMER RUN

Wading thigh-deep,
I cast a fly
which I tied last winter,
and let it drift
below the riffle.

There, a steelhead lies,
weighing the current,
balancing in one place,
the mouth slowly working
open and closed.

While eyes that have never known sleep
signal the body to rise,
slide steadily forward,
shadow flickering
over mossy stones.

In a smooth flash of motion,
deft as a blade, the fish strikes
and the surface explodes.

Trembling violently in air,
amid spray and foam,
the steelhead blazes like a mirror catching sun,
falls back, extinguishing the fire,
only to lift again,
a flame out of water.

In a long meteoric arc,
cutting a vee across the surface,
the fish unable to dislodge the hook,
dashes instinctively down stream.

Zigzagging back and forth,
fighting the current and line,
it is only a matter of time,
until this miracle of energy
rests on its side,
gills flaring.

She's fat with roe,
so I work the barb out
and let her go
on her journey
from which
there is no escape.

CLAMMING

I tote a long blade shovel
and bring a bucket
to where the tide
like a sheet rolls back
exposing the soft beach.

Walk quiet, or they can hear me.
The ground has ears.

I scout the sand
for bubbles, a diver's oxygen
breaking the surface . . .

And spotting one,
commence to digging: gold fever,
Katmandu.

At the first sound, that fella takes off
mole quick.

He's already a mile ahead, so I go
to using my hands
as if remembering
a bone. Then reach, fingers searching
for the valve—grab hold
and dredge up
this razor clam.

When I've captured enough,
I'll dig a pit, line it with stones
the way the Indians did. Toss in driftwood
that burns down to coals, heat wrinkling the air
like furrows across a dune. The clams bake
covered beneath seaweed. What I can't eat,
I throw to a spiral of huge and noisy gulls.

SILETZ

Having risen, they fall,
toppled by harsh wind or time.
Those that splash into the river
grate over boulders, snapping limbs.

The logs float for days
finding their way to the bay
and beach up like canoes.

Scattered across mudflats,
snags anchor, grow pine.
Others drift, roll up on the spit,
a frenzy of tangled bones.

White as this wood, full moon after first snow
is the signal to light a bonfire,
to chant and do the heron dance.

The old stories will be told
while coals, eyes of animals
blink in the dark.

PACIFIC COAST QUAKE

9.0 January 26, 1700

The ground began to shake as if Thunderbird and Orca
were having a colossal battle. Along bays, forests toppled
like dropped bundles of sticks.

Indians heard lodge and ridge poles crack,
felt the bitter rush of air, rain,
when roofs collapsed.

Those closest to beaches listened to the ocean
make a strange sucking roar,
a monster not heard or seen before,

while the tidal wave gathered more than thirty feet tall—
smashing into cliffs and dunes, driving the surge
more than a mile past shore.

The Tillamook lost masks, robes, ceremonial clothes,
fishing lines and hooks, the winter's supply of wood
scattered and buried like shells on a beach.

Drenched and shaking, there was nothing dry to start a fire.
Those with families farther up river, stumbled their way
along dark paths.

While others staying by the bodies of loved ones
waited for faint light to seep over mountain forests
and ravens sing their waking songs.

NEWPORT

In an obscure history book, I read
that U.S. Army troops built the blockhouse
on top of the Yaquina's burial ground.

Many times I have walked down
the wide curving path to the beach.
On this trail soldiers hauled
over fifty burial canoes
to the water's edge,
setting them adrift
on the outgoing tide.

For most of the day, the waves were calm,
and the dugouts like a broken log boom
began to drift slowly apart. By late afternoon,
wind rising, the tribe watched in horror
as a curl of a wave caught a canoe sideways
tipping it over.

As though they possessed the eyes of the dead,
the entire village stared, almost hypnotized.
They had to restrain their rage—
prisoners on their own land.
The sergeant and his men
holding rifles loaded and ready
for any problem.

Each canoe, a cradle,
rocking with the waves
might only last a few hours—a few days,
then capsize or swamp,
be ground to bits on coastal rocks,
or tossed up on a beach
like driftwood during a storm.

Sitting on the dunes,
the families watched the sun
sink slowly on the horizon,
until the last rays of light went dim,
and it became too difficult to see
the debris spreading across
the dark windswept ocean.

THE OCTOPUS TREE

Down from a dull gray sky,
drizzle falls cold and steady.
What light filters through the canopy of limbs
is soft and dim as sitting in a church.
Inside each canoe they would place a bowl of water
with strips of pemmican for the long journey.

Branches have endured so many
every tentacle is permanently bent
like an old man's back.

The Tillamook say the great Sitka Spruce
has been here since the beginning.
The tree sings the cradle song
rocking in the wind.

ENCOUNTER

Emerging from mist, two field hawks
make a slow circular descent
as though sliding down
a spiral staircase.

Instead of riding thermals or hunting mice,
they glide lower than tree tops,
calling to each other,
sinking steadily to eye level.

Wheeling about me, they move gracefully
on opposite sides of the circle.
As in a trance, my golden retriever
is riveted to their orbits and neglects to bark.

Revolving around us, the redtails
gradually begin to circle higher,
ascending like souls,
until they vanish into fog.

The strength of their wings sweeping the air is gone,
but burns clear in my memory.
The glint of sky reflecting in their eyes.
The light sifting from heaven.

BORN IN OREGON

Some days I am a fir. Squirrels eat from my limbs.
Other days I am a rhododendron. My genes are coded
as cuneiform. Toadstools and moss grow in the caverns
of my lungs. I am accustomed to the sky,
gray as wax paper.

BLACKBERRY SEASON

My custom is to cut the top off a milk carton,
bore two holes, and thread a piece of string.

Wearing it like a necklace, I walk down the road
to my favorite patch that guards an abandoned barn.

Some berries are still green, while others hang
succulent, so sweet hornets become drunk.

To reach the largest constellations,
my feet step on vines, barbed dragon tails.

Crows scold me for taking their dinner.
A browsing doe does not seem to mind.

On sultry nights, the ripe scent will drift for miles.
I dream them piled on vanilla ice cream or stuffed in pies.

This one is so plump, the mere plucking
crushes it between thumb and forefinger.

I fill the container full and empty them
into a stainless steel bowl.

Raising a berry to my lips,
the taste lingers like a good kiss.

FULL MOON, CLEAR SKY

I stand in the shadows on the back deck
and scan the far edges of the field—
ripe wheat, a shimmering lake.

Wading towards me
a doe emerges, shaking herself clean,
shedding grain like droplets.

She steps into my wife's garden
and feasts on carrot tops, snow peas.

Then, a cacophony of yelping
echoes out of the woods. Coyotes
fighting over a kill.

She plunges into the field
and races in the opposite direction.

As quickly as the commotion began, it ends.
The night recedes, shrinking back
to its original shape
of crickets, stars,
the wind.

AMONG THESE HILLS

Walking the fields
I might find their tracks.

In town an ambulance plays its siren.
Maybe someone having a heart attack.

Over the next rise, high-pitched howls
answer back.

Some nights, it does not take long
for the pack to begin

intoning, one higher than another,
so a few sound like a choir.

In the fall, when loggers burn slash
and the crests of clear-cuts glow,

they call to each other,
letting everyone know there is danger.

HARVEST

High in a fir, a red-tailed hawk perches on a limb.
Facing into the wind, she preens
while observing barn swallows dip and swerve,
taking insects from the freshly mown field.

When the breeze sets the tree to swaying,
she rises on her legs, wings spread
to gain balance once more, and waits patiently
for the tractor cutting hay to draw closer.

Before the machinery clatters by,
the hawk launches into air, gives three long medium whistles,
and suspended on thermals,
floats in an effortless circle.

The farmer, in the middle of a sphere of noise,
is unaware that the blades have flushed a shrew.
It scampers, zigzagging, then hesitates, heartbeat
loud behind its ears, only to run again, unsure . . .

Wings tucked, talons extended, the bird dives
as though gliding down a curved slide. In one violent surge,
spurs sink into fur. She pecks once, twice,
and lifts her wings for the evergreen, where

she tears the viscera from bone,
lets the skull fall through branches
like a pine cone, and watches the farmer
turn around at the end of the field.

DEER AMONG BLUE WOODS

I rest on top of Father's shoulders,
my gloves clutching the earmuffs of his winter cap.

With every long stride,
we glide over the frozen earth.

Attached to the horizon, our profiles blend with fog.
The dark plowed field holds us to this reality.

At the edge of the blue woods, there are a dozen deer.
They lift their heads, turn delicate ears.

Standing still, we breathe so shallow
our breath clouds no longer mingle.

The deer separate from shadows
and go on browsing.

When the wind shifts,
they fade nebulously into the woods . . .

Decades later, I return with a daughter
on top of my shoulders.

The deer, as though they are phantoms,
appear out of fog.

Father, I think of you often . . .
silhouettes on the horizon again.

FREEZING MOON

Through a windswept field, champagne powder blows.
I walk on sculptured dunes toward the vacant road
and pause to pick up a maple seed
still attached to its wing.

There are no maples for miles.
Maybe it was dropped by a sparrow flying home.

Using the heel of my boot as a hoe,
I scrape away a crust of ice
and plant this seed under a thin layer of soil,
so that come spring
a tree might break from the ground . . .

rising into the air out of which it fell,
and on another night such as this
will hold the moonlight
in the snow on its branches.

MIDWINTER: SAUVIE ISLAND

In late afternoon, sunlight
slices between huge gray clouds
turning the valley and hills vibrant.
All colors grow equally intense
as if someone is adjusting a dial.

Each hue threatens to spill out
of the physical shape it possesses:
forest, fields, and houses
becoming a giant tide.

Across the uplands, vanes of geese
populate the air: so many
filling a piece of sky,
the eye can not count them.

Calling hungrily to each other,
they begin a large sweeping circle
for their gradual approach . . .

Flock after flock skim over tree tops,
then descend, glide in, and just before touching down
beat wings—rowing the air—finally to settle
into wheat stubble.

Clouds heal together. Light fades.
What seems so vivid drains away.
For the first time, the geese are silent.
Some feed. Others tuck their heads beneath bent wings—
the ancestral messages of distant landmarks
surfacing and sinking in their blood.

OREGON RAIN

The rain trampolines on a spider's web, glistens
on the fur of a muskrat crossing the road,
bounces off the pavement like grease in a hot skillet.

The rain falls in the sleep of wheat farmers,
pulled by gravity through diaphanous spaces,
beading on umbrellas, faces cursing its name.

The rain changes to snow, white swans,
and back to rain before disappearing
into the fire.

The rain, an affliction, seeps between bones,
stiffens the joints, breaks the sun into ribbons,
becomes a word and the word evaporates on the tongue.

The rain washes volcanic dust down gutters,
drips from the cold chimney, taps methodically,
a pulse filling a bucket that must be emptied every morning.

MT. ST. HELENS: INSIDE THE BLAST ZONE

Decimated by five hundred Hiroshimas,
the forest is gone . . .

Wherever I step,
ash, finer than ground glass, roils up . . .

In this graveyard, there is not a branch
for the wind to ruffle.

There are more downed trees
than the eye can count,

more logs in Spirit Lake
than any beaver could possibly dream.

Hemlock, spruce, and fir, stripped of bark, gray as driftwood,
lie on hillsides like quills on a porcupine's back.

In gullies, where snow shrouds melt, lichen sprout.
If enough dust blows away, fireweed burrows out.

I leave footprints
like Armstrong did on the moon.

At my feet, a spider, the size of an asterisk,
crawls over sand . . .

to begin again
start with small things.

II

In the Cascades

The clearest way into the Universe
is through a forest wilderness.

John Muir

IN THE SILENCE OF A PINE CONE FALLING

Cones, ripe, choose their own moment:
a summer lightning flash,
a snowstorm in July, whenever
no one is looking.

Unconcerned with the physics of flight,
they spiral down,
scattering sparks
to grow from a graveyard of snags,
fractured bones.

If not eaten by chipmunks,
Canadian jays, or carried away
by ants, these seeds sprout:
record their birthfall—years
calibrated with each new ring
where time forms
concentric circles
like the universe.

The forest does not begin or end,
reconstructing itself again and again—
a silent explosion
continually rising.

Seed sprouting seed,
rains down to become a Chehalem drum,
a canoe gliding across a snow fed lake,
wood that burns, like lovers, long into the night.

MIRROR IN THE FOREST

Through the forest, shafts of light fall
forming a geometry of shadows.

I huddle by the campfire and listen
to jays sing their waking songs.

From a rusty spike embedded into bark
hangs a mirror which holds a face:

Grandfather dabbing shaving cream
on whiskers.

Delicately he holds the razor. Afternoons,
both hands swing a sledgehammer,

splitting cross sections of hemlock and fir
with an iron wedge that gleams

like a bar of silver
sliding between sapwood.

Five years old, full of questions, I
watch him, watch himself shave—

skinning his winter beard
as though clear-cutting a stand of timber.

I ask him how sharp is the blade.
He puts some cream on my cheek

and offers me a shave.
I run far enough away

that he turns back
to his reflection.

I return three decades later
to build another fire in the stone ring

and wipe the mirror clean
of all the lost years.

IN THE DESCHUTES

I walk this mountain trail
with black powder on my back,
blasting caps in both hands,

a killer
of stumps,

a maker
of pits.

Shovel dirt,
plant the charge,
string wire behind a tree,
yell,

    Fire in the hole!

A chipmunk takes shelter.

    Fire in the hole!

A blue jay mocks.

    Fire in the hole!

I touch it off,

and where the stump used to be,

the sun
as through a high church window
suspends dust.

WESTFIR

They were born here.
The fire chief delivered them
on a makeshift table in the station.
Since their fathers went to work in the sawmill,
they went to work in the sawmill.
When the economy wore thin,
unraveling easily as an old rope,
the mill shut down. Five years later,
the men still sit home or in the bars,
waiting out the winter like fishermen.
Many have never left this town.
Many will never leave.
The graveyard is full of small imaginations.

BLACK CANYON

The wind, a heron, lifting off the river
makes the leaves flutter
so light speckles over the path.

I climb down the bank holding on to roots,
exposed nerves, teeter over flat gray stones
ripe with dead moss where trout made their homes,

wade waist deep, and submerge into glacial chill.
I shed sight, smell, the dust
from cutting wood all day.

Stair steps of basalt escarpments,
ledges of bedrock rise above me.
I begin kicking towards the far shore.

If I could swim where the river has been,
I would float with the red-tailed hawk,
no shadow, no weight,

my reflection consumed
by a multitude of flames
blazing on the water.

MEDITATION IN A LOOKOUT TOWER

Seeing the flash, begin counting, *one thousand one,*
one thousand two . . .

The storm, primordial, spiderwebs across ridges.
When thunder rolls, the air torn, sews back together.

Hammered by the jolt, the concussion—
this tiny cabin rattles and shakes, an earthquake.

Stay perched on the wooden kitchen stool
with blue glass telegraph insulators cupping its feet.

Sleep is not an option. Even if reclining were possible,
the bunk has box springs which can conduct electricity.

Don't get between two metal objects.
Lightning can jump, pass through a person like a laser.

A spotter can see into the nooks and crevices of valleys
satellite imagery can't detect.

A fire can smolder for days. Wisps of smoke, dragon's breath,
might only be seen during the first hour of dawn's slanting light.

The Klamath believed that fire lived inside a tree
somewhere deep in the forest.

AERIAL DELIVERY: BOMBING THE CASCADES

Skimming firs,
a multitude under my wings,
I push the button
dropping three thousand
rainbow, brook, golden, cutthroat:
a cloudburst of fingerlings
into a lake
wide as a village.

Christ, eyes lifted,
could pull down salmon.
Showering silver—
atoms—
carp and perch
ascended from the ponds.

Shaped like Japanese lanterns,
the paper balloons: incendiary bombs, migrated
across the Pacific
to spawn fire
in the timber.

The plane trembles—flickering trout
somersault out
ricocheting through
a reflection of sky.

SHELTER COVE

The cabin hibernates under snow.
I tunnel out, feed bread crumbs
to juncos, towhees, Canadian jays.
The sun burns inside each crystal
on the lake. Ice has fractured
the dock like bone. Years ago,
workmen on the railroad
cut blocks for refrigeration.
Mules and wagons sometimes disappeared
under the weight.

CONSTRUCTING CLOCKS

When moonlight skates on the frozen lake,
my hands shape pieces to fit.

The cogs are fashioned out of scraps of metal
hauled back from the dump.

For faces, I scavenge the forest for burls
off old stumps.

Cut and polished,
they shine like thunder eggs.

Bending strips from herring and ham cans
to gain the right tension, my fingers load each spring.

By now, almost morning, the kerosene burning low,
the clock sings its first song.

The pendulum swings
where the last second was . . .

soothing as the soft tick of snowmelt
dripping off fir boughs,

or my rocking chair moving back and forth
until I close my eyes and fall asleep.

THAWING OUT

Under a thin layer of ice,
my head contains the lake,

brimming with light
that is hatching
steadily alive.

Hives of mosquitoes
mill the air,

where snow dissolves
like a memory

the sun is patient.

I walk down
through galaxies of anemone,
sword fern, lupine,

watch wind
carve patterns on the lake
and wait for the evening crickets.

ODELL LAKE

Water laps
a steady pulse.

The lines are slack
as our luck.

I lean over the bow
and whisper
to mackinaw
and kokanee
the story of my life.

I exaggerate
in all the appropriate places.

It does no good.

Sun shafting past
my shadow
drives them deep.

NISHAWAKA CREEK

Blueberries, indigo planets, so ripe
that plucking them from the branches
my hands become stained, fingerprinted.

The best ones grow closest
to the stream. Grizzlies came
for spawning salmon. Indians collected dye.
Pioneers ran traplines, snaring mink,
ermine, lynx.

I come for breakfast. Hummingbirds
skim bushes patched with sunlight.
Like remnants of snow
in fir shadows, my hunger
has almost disappeared.

SUMMIT LAKE

When snow melts, green mountains slope
to the cabin's door. I reach for my pole,
its lures like sparkling ornaments
and mosquitoes droning a distant highway,
hike down to shore.

Dragonflies, small black kites, hover
above the boat. I drift
wherever
slow currents
take me. Firs part
at the bow, slide together under stern.
I drop hook and worm, settle back,
wait for the pull.

MYSTERY

In the deepest part of Odell Lake
an archaeologist scuba diving found
four lava bowls buried in silt.

Each one has a hole
the size of a walnut
drilled neatly in the bottom.

Maybe the Klamath used them to anchor canoes
or the Modocs "killed" the bowls
as a sacrifice, so the objects' souls
would join the spirit of a dead chief.

No one knows for sure. Maybe
there was a woman named Tired-of-Cooking.
She became unhappy that nobody helped her
or said thank you.

During the night, while everyone was sleeping,
Tired-of-Cooking went down to the shore
and after drilling the holes,
bent back birch
and catapulted
every bowl
into the lake.

In the morning, when the camp assembled to eat,
Tired-of-Cooking told them
there would be no food
until new bowls were made
or iron kettles bought
from French trappers.

Trickster came in the dark
and stole the bowls
to cook his dinner.

SKYLINE TRAIL

After dawn, I hike through shadows of pine.
With each step, small puffs of pumice dust rise.

The path, a dim memory, fades with every passing year.
Pine needles and windfalls erase that anyone was here.

In thin brilliant mountain air, I pause to catch my breath.
Any mosquito landing on my arms meets a quick death.

Further up the trail, I kneel at a fast flowing creek,
glacial ice which melted at eight thousand feet,

sings as water ribbons among boulders—
shimmering fabric tearing and mending back together.

I cup my hands and drink in cold light, until fingers go numb.
Bees pollinating alpine yellow mimulus faintly hum.

Along the far bank, a few strawberries grow.
They will not flourish again before winter's shroud of snow.

Folding the frayed map, I follow this forgotten black line,
which continues to twist, turn, climb.

BLOWDOWN

In high winds and wet soil, some crash down
pulling up roots like Medusa's hair.
Others topple under the weight of snow,
buckling, full of rot.

And those struck by lightning
or another tree on its way down
have splintered trunks, twisted and snapped
as if hit by artillery fire.

I walk the backs of these giants
which fell—exploding like thunder,
balance on each pillar, using them for bridges
through brush and over cascading streams.

Sometimes, mushrooms, half-moons,
grow along their sides,
or there are holes
where a woodpecker hammered termites.

Over decades, a fir will slowly submerge
into pumice and debris . . .
become a home
for ants, grubs, a nest of bees.

Then there are a few mantled in moss
where seedlings sprout, sails on a ship,
and what is left gradually disappears
into the forest floor, sinking below a new horizon.

SERENITY BAY, ODELL LAKE

A deer wades in the shallows at dusk.
The lake is smooth and calm as a meditation.

Trout sporadically rise
taking flies, forming rings . . .

While evening dims, shadows
the size of a hand, flit across the surface.

Seizing insects, they dive in looping figure eights
or slightly graze the water,

forming ripples, which blend
back into the transparent body

already turning a black sheen,
capturing stars, galaxies—

light from across the universe
before the Cascades existed.

EAGLE ROCK

Hiking the crest of the ridge,
I rest where the trail pauses.

Manzanita sculptures through shale
while polemoniums grip any foothold they can find.

A cold mist, almost weightless, drifts
out of the soft glow of overcast.

Water sequins moss, drips off
fir boughs and is soaked up
by pumice turning gold.

Far below, not one fishing boat trolls the lake.
Smoke from campfires rises like fog.

The voice in my step
dissolves into damp undergrowth.
I have no reason to speak.

FIREWOOD

Splitting the log, my axe echoes fall
through trees. Beneath bark
rings chart long winters.

Each stroke delivered, fir rips open
and a few decades splinter, then lay in the dust.

I fill the old milk crate with four gallons of wood,
haul the load inside, place handfuls of kindling
on the grate.

The coals flare, faintly hissing,
alchemizing earth into air.

Heat spreads across the room
dissipating the chill from my clothes.
I stare at the flames . . .

charcoal drawings of wildcat, deer, and bear,
indelibly carved in the walls of memory—

Smoke, like cloth, unravels up the chimney
to tangle among the highest limbs and vanish
against the gray diminishing afternoon.

CLEAR LAKE

High above the ancient tree tops,
my rowboat floats
on a mirror of sky,

while I dream of how lava must have roiled
from the South Sister
sealing off the valley,

and streams having no place to flow
slowly backed up, drowning the forest
beneath me.

Now petrified,
these firs rise like spires
out of the pumice and silt.

They were alive before the Romans and Greeks,
even before the great pyramids
were built.

Where once there was wind
the slow steady tug of current
can not bend them.

Instead of blue jays,
rainbow trout glide
from tree to tree.

I bait my hook with half a worm, drop it carefully
over the side, and watch it descend
into a reflection of a snow-covered peak.

MCKENZIE RIVER

Pulling a few short strokes with the left oar,
I position myself between outcroppings of basalt,

tall and wide as two story houses,
and I am in the slick—

slide down the chute, plunging
into a hole so deep I strike bottom.

Wave higher than my head,
the raft rockets up and over.

Bucking white water,
the bow rises and falls, a seesaw.

Blasting through crest after crest,
spray explodes, raining shrapnel.

Wooden driftboats never make it through these rapids.
Boulders grind them to shreds.

If caught in a curl back, they capsize and spin
like a turning on a lathe.

I stair-step down through riffles
into a large turquoise pool

where salmon remain cool
during long sweltering afternoons.

When the resonance of crashing water begins to cease,
the boat floats slow as a willow leaf.

Kingfishers thread the air and dive.
Mossy stones slide by.

Lifting dripping oars, I settle back
into the easy pace of the current's momentum,

while the day slips past
like so much debris.

UNCLE ERIC'S FISHING TIPS

Trolling along the shore, our boat lightly buffets
windrows of sun speckled water.

The lure skimming weeds taunts them
with the hypnotic flash of a minnow.

Here, the lake is so shallow, I spot trout
grazing on the bottom.

To help relieve the tedium of waiting, I read the sports,
comics, and work my way backwards through world news.

Eric sings parts of songs
that were popular in the forties.

I don't recognize any of the melodies,
but the fish seem to like it.

By the time he finishes the last chorus,
he will have hooked another and be reeling in.

Eric tells me, you have got to hold your mouth just right,
and don't think about them too much or a rainbow won't bite.

Out of the hands, vibrations flow down the pole
and into the line, sure as you called them on the phone.

So, lean your rod in a holder. Eat caviar.
Fix a tuna sandwich. Swallow a sardine.

Show them they're not so special. Even if you get skunked,
you'll go home with fish on your breath.

CATCHING THE LIMIT

I troll along the south shore,
where other fishermen say
the angling is no good: too shallow,
too many weeds. With their fish finders,
they cluster off Princess Creek,
but I don't see them catching anything.

The lake lies flat mirroring sky.
An osprey rides the currents,
until he spies a trout,
folds his wings and drops
like a swift mountain stream
falling over the edge of a cliff,
plunging talons first
into his own reflection . . .

Emerging in a fury of spray,
wings widespread, using them as oars,
the bird strokes against the surface,
flapping steadily to reach the air again,
nosing his wriggling prey into the wind.

I point the bow at the spot
where the osprey caught the rainbow.
More times than not, that is the place
my pole starts to bend.

ON THE DOCK AT EVENING

The lake and sky gradually darken.
The highest peaks hold the sun.

All the fishing boats have gone home.

A trout lifts miraculously out of the water . . .
another and another, until there is a brief flurry.

Where I laid my morning catch,
scales flake off the wood: stars,
whole galaxies moving further apart.

I have lived my life for just this moment.

CABIN FEVER

Rain pummels the roof like birdshot.
The ground is pasted with pine needles.
Water drips off enormous trees.

After a week of steady downpour,
anxiety, a squirrel trapped in the attic,
races through me.

Not wanting to fight a cold wind
or get drenched, I am down
to my last trout.

So much static on the radio,
I crank up the Victrola
and sing along, "Toot, Toot, Tootsie good-bye."

Sometimes, I stare at bear prints
on the ceiling: Ursa Major
walking across the sky.

(A grizzly came into camp,
stepped in a bucket of resin
and left his tracks.)

All morning, the men laughed,
nailing those boards
to cover beams.

These long afternoons, my hands whittle
balsa wood, glue logs together,
cut doors and windows.

Building the fireplace again,
I press small pebbles from the lake
into mortar.

Everything is to scale:
my knife, fork,
a loaf of bread.

I even paint bear prints on the ceiling,
place a figurine making a model
inside the model.

The only thing missing is the rain,
inevitable as time, dripping off
cedar shingles.

AFTER THE DOWNPOUR

I walk out on damp gray boards of the dock.
A trout slides through my reflection.

More thunderheads, billowing mountains,
approach from the west.

Kneeling in the rowboat with a coffee can,
I bail a pound of rain.

A mallard and three hens
armada along the bay.

I rest my fishing pole against the bow,
lift the oars and follow in their wake.

Ripples break from the stern,
form a V.

We float across the tops of firs
and a white peak.

Grandfather saw lightning
strike the lake.

Kokanee drift to the surface . . .
eagles, clairvoyant, appear and feast.

Fishhooks are my claws
to pull one from the deep.

PAINTING THE BOAT

Through a hot afternoon, in the shade of giant firs
Grandfather and I dip into cans of aqua blue,
lovingly painting this wood that kokanee see
while being reeled to the surface,
the wood buffeted by whitecaps that keeps us afloat,
the wood we sawed and shaped that always brings us home.

In mid-brush stroke, the cries of children reverberate
off the water down by the dock—not those at play,
but groping for a last breath. Bent over our work,
we both stand erect at the same moment, straining our ears
as though we are hunters unsure of what we first hear.

Before either of us can speak, I am running, paintbrush
dropped in the dust like a player leaving his bat at the plate,
racing along the path that leads to the lake,
thoughts flashing . . . *dive in, save them.*

Discarding my shirt, wallet, car keys, in a flailing striptease,
my feet pound the sun bleached boards of the dock. My eyes swivel
hoping for a glimpse of those I have come to rescue
before they are erased from the surface,
submerged for the last time.

At the edge, instead of launching a dive, I stop short
like coming up fast on a red light. Below, on the water,
five loons plaintively call . . .

(It is the first and last time, I have ever seen them.)
Grandfather shakes his head and slaps me on the back.
We begin to laugh—the fear draining out of us.
Still chuckling, he helps me pick up my things
as we go to finish the boat.

INHERITANCE

In Grandfather's shop, I search for a pair of gloves,
but none seem to match. Either the right or left
has been lost in an act of forgetfulness.

I find a few that could be sculptures Rodin would have admired:
a hand gripping an invisible hammer, another resting as in a lap,
one pointing like it knew the correct direction.

His daily sweat soaked into the leather
making the palms shiny as calluses, fingers ridged
until stretched like skin, worn again.

I try them on and my fingerprints embed
on top of his. My hands ready to rake twigs and cones
blown down around the cabin all winter.

ROUGH WIND

You can tell when something's coming.
If you stop intellectualizing
one second, your nose will warn you
she's out there
bigger than any bear
or woman
you would want to tangle with
after you came home
one time too many, too late.

It's that old cricket in the box,
the barometer in an arthritic knee,
but if you don't have either
of those, notice
the blue jay stopped complaining
and a chipmunk is scarce
as a lumberjack around a skunk.

Hear it? Far off at first,
a long freight
pulling a steep grade.
Now closer, a teakettle
beginning to vibrate
while the burner heats
on the stove. Time to go
inside, sit by the fire.

A door in the sky
is thrown open. Fir boughs
sway up and down
like a flock
of huge birds.

The boats drum
against the docks.

I've seen cabins
that have been axed
by a tree. The roof and beams
cut clean
as if with a Homelite.

Behind my place
there were two evergreens
which given a push
could have toppled
severing the ridgepole.

I fell, bucked, split, and stacked them
on the back porch. The wood smells
like the forest after a dismal rain.
Pitch, honey thick, seeps
from under the bark.

MOVING INTO NIGHT

After dinner dishes have been washed and put away,
I walk down to the dock.

Clouds hover against snow-capped peaks.
The sun, already below the horizon, turns glaciers pink.

Shadows stretch across the hills
like blankets being drawn up for the night.

Along the distant shore,
one last fisherman trolls for kokanee . . .

Below my feet, trout meander between pilings—
glide over dappled stones.

The moon rises. On the water,
it is shattered by each wave.

With cupped hands, I scoop up a brilliant shard
and wash my face with wet light.

Soon, the wind dies, and the moon is again whole.
Pale stars, floating lanterns, dot the lake.

I untie my boat, shove off,
and lifting the oars, row across the heavens.

ABOUT THE AUTHOR

MARK THALMAN's poetry has been widely published in small presses, college reviews, anthologies, and e-zines for the last three decades. His work has appeared in *Carolina Quarterly*, *CutBank*, *Many Mountains Moving*, *Natural Bridge*, *Pedestal Magazine*, and *Pennsylvania Review*, among others. He received his Master of Fine Arts in Creative Writing from the University of Oregon, and he teaches English in the public schools. Thalman has been an Assistant Poetry Editor for the *Northwest Review*, a Poet-in-the-Schools for the Oregon Art Commission, an Instructor for Chemeketa Community College, and a board member of the Portland Poetry Festival. Thalman was born and raised in Eugene and now resides in Forest Grove, Oregon, with his wife and their two golden retrievers, Sherlock Holmes and Agatha Christie. For more information please visit markthalman.com.

ABOUT THE PUBLISHER

Bedbug Press was founded in 1995 by the late Tony Gorsline, who had a lifelong love of books and writing. Under the imprints Cloudbank Books and Fairweather Books, Bedbug Press published fifteen books of poetry, a creative nonfiction memoir, and a series of children's coloring books.

In 2003, the press established The Northwest Poetry Series with the publication of *My Problem with the Truth* by Chris Anderson. Since then, four more books by Northwest poets have been added to the series: *Insects of South Corvallis* by Charles Goodrich, *Out of Town* by Lex Runciman, *A Bride of Narrow Escape* by Paulann Petersen, and *Catching the Limit* by Mark Thalman.

Also in 2003, the press began an annual poetry contest, The Rhea & Seymour Gorsline Poetry Competition. The contest offers a cash prize and publication of the winning manuscript. *Textbook Illustrations of the Human Body* by George Estreich (Corvallis, OR) was the winner of the 2003 contest. *Solar Prominence* by Kevin Craft (Seattle, WA) was the 2004 winner, *Gathering Sound* by Susan Davis (Chapel Hill, NC) and *Friday and the Year That Followed* by Juan J. Morales (Pueblo, CO) were cowinners of the 2005 prize, and *Heaven of the Moment* by John C. Morrison (Portland, OR) was the 2006 prizewinner.

Bedbug Press authors have received a number of honors: Barbara Koons (*Night Highway*), first finalist for the 2006 Best Books of Indiana Awards; David Hassler (*Red Kimono, Yellow Barn*), 2006 Ohio Poet of the Year; Paulann Petersen (*A Bride of Narrow Escape*), recipient of the Stewart H. Holbrook Literary Legacy Award and a finalist for the 2006 Oregon Literary Arts Oregon Book Award for Poetry; Freddy Frankel (*In a Stone's Hollow*), recipient of the New England Writers Robert Penn Warren First Award in 2003; and the late Dorinda Clifton (*Woman in the Water: A Memoir of Growing Up in Hollywoodland*), featured at the 2006 Memphis Film Festival and recipient of fellowships to the MacDowell Colony.

It is our hope that all our books express a commitment to quality in writing and publishing.

COLOPHON

Titles and text are set in Adobe Garamond 3.
Typeset by Imprint Services, Corvallis, Oregon.